Table of Terminology Contents

Introduction

Technology is all around us in today's fast-paced world, making our lives easier and more connected than ever. But it's simple to feel left behind with all the new terminology and phrases that are being used. For anyone who wants to easily traverse the world of technology, "Crack the Tech Code: A Simplified Guide to Technology Terms" is the ideal book. This book will enable you to discover the mysteries of the tech world and master the lingo of the digital era, whether you're a tech novice or a seasoned pro. Each concept used in this book is explained using the ELI5 (Explain like I'm five) method.

Explain like I'm five:

"Crack the Tech Code" is a special book that helps explain all the hard words about technology in an easy way. It's like a magic key that helps you understand the tech world better.

Extended Reality

The term "Extended Reality" (XR), which has gained popularity, refers to a range of immersive technologies that aim to obfuscate the boundaries between the real and virtual worlds. Virtual Reality (VR), Augmented Reality (AR), and Mixed Reality are all immersive technologies that fall under the general term "XR" (MR).

Virtual Reality (VR) is an entirely artificial environment that submerges people in a virtual setting. Users put on a headset that covers their eyes, ears, and, in some situations, other body parts like the hands or feet in order to enjoy virtual reality. The user gets a 360-degree picture of a digital environment that reacts to their movements and actions, giving them the impression that they are actually there. Virtual reality (VR) is frequently utilized in gaming, where the technology may offer a fully immersive experience that enables users to interact with virtual worlds in previously impractical ways. It can produce accurate simulations of risky or complicated environments, making it useful in education and training.

In augmented reality (AR), digital data is superimposed over the user's actual environment. A wearable gadget like smart glasses or the camera on a smartphone can be used to experience augmented reality. By adding virtual items or information to the real-world surroundings, the device creates the illusion that the virtual material is actually a part of the physical world. In marketing and advertising, augmented reality is frequently utilized to give customers interactive product demos or improve the buying experience. It is employed in education as well, where it can give pupils intriguing and dynamic learning opportunities.

AR and VR components coexist in mixed reality (MR). It creates a smooth and immersive experience by fusing real-world elements with digital ones. Digital objects that appear to be physically present in the real world can respond to the user's surroundings in the real world and can be interacted with by users. MR is frequently employed in manufacturing and industry, where it can give employees virtual training and simulations of challenging or dangerous conditions. Additionally, it is employed in gaming and entertainment, where it can offer customers one-of-a-kind, captivating experiences that blend digital and physical components.

The uses for XR are numerous and diverse, and they develop and grow more and more each day. Industries like healthcare, education, manufacturing, and entertainment might all be revolutionized by XR. In the field of healthcare, XR can be used to train medical staff, replicate medical procedures, and assist patients in overcoming trauma or phobias. In the classroom, XR can be utilized to provide engaging interactive learning experiences that help students better understand difficult subjects. To increase safety and productivity in the industrial industry, XR can be used to give employees virtual training and simulations of challenging or dangerous conditions.

Working with XR technology has a number of difficulties and constraints, though. The expensive price of hardware and software is one of the key obstacles, and it may restrict the use of XR by a larger group of people. Another difficulty is the potential for sensory overload, which may make some users feel uncomfortable or confused. However, XR technology creates significant ethical issues, such as the risk of addiction or its effects on interpersonal relationships.

In conclusion, Extended Reality (XR) is a potent and adaptable technology that has the potential to change how we engage with the environment. XR is creating new possibilities for creativity, learning, and discovery by obfuscating the lines between the physical and digital worlds. Even though there are obstacles and restrictions that must be overcome, XR offers a wide range of intriguing possibilities that will continue to influence technology for many years to come.

Explain XR like I'm five:

XR refers to the use of specialized technology to create the illusion that you are somewhere else. It's as if you're holding up a special object or wearing special glasses that appear to show you things that aren't actually there. It's an enjoyable way to play games or discover new stuff!

Avatar

The term "avatar" comes from Hindu mythology, where it designates a god or goddess who has taken human form. A graphic depiction of a user or individual in a virtual environment is known as an avatar in modern technology. In a variety of contexts, including social media and online communities as well as video games and virtual reality, avatars can be tailored to resemble the user or a fictional character.

Since the 1980s, when they first appeared in video games, avatars have been a thing. The player's character in the game world was represented by an avatar in these early games. Avatars are being used in a variety of technological contexts, including virtual reality, augmented reality, and online communities.

In recent years, using avatars in virtual reality environments has become one of the most common practices. Avatars are employed in these settings to represent the user's presence in the virtual world, enabling more immersive interactions with other users and virtual items. Users can create fictional characters to represent themselves in the digital realm or alter their avatars to appear like them.

The use of avatars is also widespread in online gaming groups. To represent their characters in the game world, gamers can design and personalize their avatars. In doing so, users can develop a distinctive persona and tailor their gaming experience. In certain games, avatars can even interact with other players nonverbally by expressing emotions or actions through gestures or facial expressions.

In addition to gaming and virtual reality, avatars are also used in other online applications such as social media and virtual meetings. In these contexts, avatars can be used to represent a user's identity in a more anonymous way. Users can choose to use a fictional avatar instead of their real identity, allowing them to participate in online communities without revealing their true identity.

Avatar use in technology also brings up moral dilemmas involving identity, privacy, and representation. In some circumstances, such as in social media or online dating, the use of avatars may result in misrepresentation or fraud. Moreover, it may foster exaggerated notions of certain groups or identities.

In spite of these reservations, avatars have permeated modern technology and digital society. They give users the opportunity to forge distinctive identities, customize their online experience, and engage in virtual social interactions. The use of avatars is projected to increase in frequency and sophistication as technology progresses, enabling more lifelike and immersive digital experiences.

The workplace is one setting where avatar use is on the rise. Avatars can be used to represent employees in virtual meetings in remote work settings, allowing for more natural and immersive communication between participants. By doing so, distant teams' collaboration and feelings of isolation may be lessened.

The usage of avatars in healthcare is another field. In telemedicine sessions, patients can be represented by avatars, enabling clinicians to consult with patients remotely without requiring their actual presence. In order to help patients better grasp their diseases and available treatments, avatars can also be utilized to give patient education and support.

Explain Avatars like I'm five:

Avatars are virtual representations of yourself that you can make in a computer program or video game. It's like creating a cartoon version of yourself that has superhuman abilities like the ability to fly or jump really high. It's entertaining to temporarily assume another person's identity by using your avatar for online communication or game play.

AI (Artificial Intelligence)

One of the most important technological advancements of the 21st century is artificial intelligence (AI). It is a broad phrase that covers a variety of computer science innovations, such as robotics, machine learning, and natural language processing. Artificial intelligence (AI) systems are made to replicate human intelligence and decision-making processes, allowing robots to complete complicated jobs with little assistance from humans.

The use of AI is already widespread, ranging from chatbots and virtual assistants to self-driving cars and medical diagnoses. AI technology has the ability to completely transform practically every sector of the economy and every aspect of our life, including healthcare, banking, transportation, and education.

The use of AI in robotics is allowing machines to carry out sophisticated tasks that were previously impossible or challenging for humans. Robots with AI can, for instance, navigate challenging surroundings, gain experience from their mistakes, and adjust to changing circumstances.

Building machines that can learn and think like humans is at the heart of artificial intelligence. Machine learning, a sort of AI that enables machines to learn from data and enhance their performance over time, is one of the most fundamental ideas in artificial intelligence. Algorithms for machine learning are created to uncover patterns in data, spot correlations, and generate predictions based on past data.

Natural language processing (NLP), which is the capacity of machines to comprehend and interpret human language, is another crucial component of AI. Chatbots, virtual assistants, and other applications that call for robots to communicate with people in a natural and intuitive way leverage NLP technology.

The potential benefits of AI are vast, but there are also significant challenges that need to be addressed. One of the main concerns about AI is the potential for job displacement, as machines are increasingly able to perform tasks that were previously done by humans. There are also concerns about the ethical implications of AI, particularly as it becomes more advanced and autonomous.

Despite these difficulties, AI is probably going to become more and more significant in our lives in the years to come. The potential applications of AI are essentially limitless, ranging from enhancing healthcare outcomes to fostering fresh kinds of creativity and innovation. In order to guarantee that this transformative technology is developed in a responsible and ethical manner as we continue to explore its potential, it is crucial to be aware of any hazards it may provide.

Explain AI like I'm five:

AI refers to the process by which we teach computers to be extremely intelligent, much like humans. With the exception of the fact that we train computers to do it as well, it is similar to learning anything new and improving over time. They have the ability to interact with humans, make choices, and even operate motor vehicles. It's awesome how AI makes our work easier and faster.

Matter

A relatively new concept in technology that is gaining use in the tech sector is "matter." It is a word used to describe a new standard for designing and generating 3D environments and objects that can be used on various platforms and gadgets. Fundamentally, matter is a fresh approach to producing and presenting 3D material that aims to be faster, more adaptable, and more widely available than conventional 3D rendering methods.

One of matter's main benefits is that it makes it possible to create 3D scenes and objects that can be used on a variety of platforms and gadgets, including smartphones, desktop computers, and virtual reality headsets. This makes it simpler for developers to create immersive 3D experiences for a larger audience because they can design once and deliver wherever.

Moreover, Matter is made to be more effective than conventional 3D rendering methods. This is accomplished by utilizing a brand-new file format called USDZ, which was created especially for the storage of 3D environments and objects. Since the USDZ format is intended for streaming and compression, 3D material may be loaded on a range of devices rapidly and effectively.

The adaptability of matter is another benefit. It can be applied to a variety of tasks, including training and teaching as well as gaming and enjoyment. Matter, for instance, can be utilized to build virtual training grounds for firefighters or medical personnel, enabling them to simulate real-world situations without endangering themselves or others.

The rising need for immersive 3D experiences across a range of sectors is one of the main forces driving the development of matter. For gaming, entertainment, and education, virtual reality and augmented reality are gaining in popularity, and more effective and adaptable 3D rendering methods are needed to enable these experiences.

There are, however, significant difficulties related to the subject. The difficulty of producing 3D content that is optimized for the matter standard is one of the major difficulties. Some developers and content producers may find this to be a hurdle because it calls for specific knowledge and equipment.

Concerns have also been raised regarding the possibility of a new type of digital divide being brought about by matter. Since matter requires specialized equipment and expertise, there is a chance that a limited number of businesses and developers may control it, limiting access and opportunity for others.

Ultimately, matter is a fascinating new advancement in immersive and 3D rendering methods. It has the ability to completely transform how we produce and consume 3D information, making it more available, effective, and adaptable than ever. It will be interesting to see how the technology is used and adopted across various industries and applications as it continues to advance.

Explain Matter like I'm five:

Making images and films that appear to be so real you could nearly touch them is called "matter." It's similar to creating a really stunning 3D image using specialized tools and computers to make it look incredibly realistic.

DLSS (Deep Learning Super Sampling)

Modern computer graphics use Deep Learning Super Sampling (DLSS), a cutting-edge technique, to improve the quality and performance of visual applications like video games. Artificial neural networks are used in DLSS, a type of machine learning, to improve the resolution and smoothness of images in real-time.

In order for DLSS to function, a high-resolution image is used as a reference, and a deep neural network is used to analyze and process the image. The neural network can then produce a new image with a greater resolution that appears smoother and more detailed than the original. To further enhance the image quality and lessen blurring or aliasing, DLSS can additionally incorporate temporal data, or information from earlier frames.

The ability of DLSS to greatly enhance video game performance on contemporary technology is one of its key advantages. By utilizing DLSS, performance can be maintained when running games at higher resolutions and with more demanding graphics settings. Without needing to upgrade their hardware, players may now take advantage of more immersive and aesthetically spectacular experiences.

DLSS also has the advantage of lowering the energy requirements of graphics-heavy applications like video games. The GPU can reduce the amount of calculations it must execute by employing DLSS, which in turn lowers power usage and heat emission.

Since DLSS is a rapidly developing technology, developers are always attempting to enhance its functionality. DLSS is projected to become an increasingly significant component of contemporary computer graphics and visual computing as more games and applications start to incorporate it.

Overall, DLSS is a groundbreaking technology that has the potential to transform the way we experience video games and other visual applications. By using advanced machine learning techniques to improve image quality and performance, DLSS is paving the way for more immersive and visually stunning experiences in the world of computer graphics.

Explain DLSS like I'm five:

DLSS is a technology that enhances the visual appeal and performance of video games on your computer. It's similar to having a mystical robot that makes the game seem even better than it already does and makes it simpler for your computer to show you all the wonderful things in the game. As a result, you may enjoy playing your favorite games even more without worrying about your computer getting too hot or slow.

Metaverse

Even before video games, movies, and literature became widely famous, there was the idea of a "Metaverse." It is a phrase used to describe a virtual environment or space where users can engage more deeply and interactively with both other users and digital items. Yet, thanks to recent technological developments, the concept of a Metaverse is becoming increasingly plausible.

The Metaverse is primarily a web-based virtual environment that allows for real-time communication with other users and virtual items. Beyond what we typically conceive of as "virtual reality" or "online gaming," it is a totally immersive experience. Users can make their own avatars, explore virtual environments, communicate with others, and engage in activities like gaming, shopping, and socializing in the Metaverse.

The Metaverse is a network of interconnected virtual environments that enables frictionless communication between people and objects, not just a single platform or application. It is an open ecosystem based on standards that enable for interoperability, enabling a variety of gadgets, platforms, and experiences.

The ability of the Metaverse to offer novel types of social contact and collaboration is one of its fundamental characteristics. The Metaverse allows users to interact with each other in a more immersive and dynamic way than standard social media platforms. This can include everything from shared gaming experiences and collaborative work settings to virtual concerts and events.

Also, the Metaverse is being considered as a potential new market for business and entrepreneurship. Users can purchase and sell virtual goods and services in a metaverse, opening up new business options for entrepreneurs and creators to develop industries centered around digital commodities and experiences.

Like with any new technology, there are worries about how the Metaverse will affect civilization. To make the Metaverse a secure and welcoming place for everyone, concerns about privacy, security, and accessibility must be addressed.

In conclusion, the Metaverse is a virtual environment that enables more immersive and engaging interactions between users and digital things. It is a networked system of virtual environments that allows for easy communication between people and things, opening up new avenues for social interaction, business, and entrepreneurship. The Metaverse has the ability to completely change how we communicate and engage with technology, despite several issues that need to be resolved.

Explain Metaverse like I'm five:

The Metaverse is kind of like a super fantastic online playground where you can make your own character, visit various locations, engage in multiplayer gaming, and even buy for items you can only obtain online. Without ever having to leave your computer or phone, it's a great place to hang out with your friends, meet new people, and do all kinds of fascinating things.

Big Data

The term "big data" refers to the enormous amounts of information that are created daily in our increasingly digitized environment. It refers to data sets that are too big and complicated for conventional data processing techniques to manage, and that demand sophisticated tools and procedures for analysis and comprehension. We'll define big data, discuss its significance, and go through some of the most essential tools and methods for managing and analyzing it.

Big data is fundamentally the ability to gather, process, and analyze enormous amounts of data in order to gain knowledge, spot trends, and improve judgment. We are creating more data than ever before thanks to the expansion of the internet, social media, and mobile devices. This information can originate from a range of sources, including posts on social media, purchases made online, sensor data, and more.

Big data is significant because it has the potential to enhance decision-making across a range of industries, including marketing, finance, healthcare, and more. Organizations can spot patterns and trends in massive datasets that might not be obvious from a smaller data set analysis. For instance, a healthcare institution might employ big data analytics to find trends in patient data that can aid in the development of new therapies, more precise illness diagnosis, and better patient outcomes.

Big data management calls for cutting-edge tools and methods created to handle the complexity and amount of the data. Storage systems, cloud computing, and distributed computing are some of the major technologies employed in big data. Organizations are now able to store and handle enormous volumes of data across numerous servers and locations thanks to these technologies.

In addition to technology, big data management and analysis require specialized knowledge and abilities. Data scientists and analysts are taught how to find patterns and trends in the data using statistical analysis and machine learning methods. To make sense of the data and convey their results to others, they may also employ visualization tools.

Machine learning, which uses algorithms to evaluate data and create predictions based on that analysis, is one of the most widely utilized big data techniques. Recommendation engines, language processing, image identification, and other activities can all be accomplished using machine learning. For instance, a recommendation engine may examine a user's purchasing patterns and provide tailored product recommendations as a result.

Big data's security and privacy practices are also crucial. Given the massive volumes of data being produced and gathered, it's crucial to make sure that it is processed and kept safely while also protecting people's privacy. Companies that gather and utilize data must abide by privacy laws like the California Consumer Privacy Act and the Global Data Protection Regulation (GDPR) (CCPA).

In summary, big data is a term used to describe the massive amounts of data being generated in our digital world. It is important because it has the potential to provide valuable insights and improve decision-making in a variety of fields. Managing and analyzing big data requires advanced technologies, specialized skills, and a focus on privacy and security. By understanding and leveraging big data, organizations can gain a competitive edge and improve outcomes in a variety of areas.

Explain Big Data like I'm five:

Huge data is similar to having a lot of information that is difficult to manage. Imagine a really large book that is so dense with words that it is difficult to read. Similar to that but with information is big data.

Big data may originate from sources other than books, such as social media, online shopping, or even simple phone use. Although all of this information can be very helpful, it is too much for one person to look at independently.

Data Mining

Finding relevant and valuable information from big volumes of data is a process known as data mining. It entails employing technology to mine data for patterns and insights that can be applied to decision-making. We will examine what data mining is, how it functions, and some of its uses in this explanation.

Let's start with a simple example to better grasp data mining. Consider that you are a store owner who is curious about the best-selling items. A lot of data is at your disposal, including details on sales, clients, and inventory. Yet, it would be extremely challenging to manually sort through all of this data and identify the information you require. Data mining can be used in this situation.

Advanced algorithms are used in data mining to examine and draw patterns from massive amounts of data. These algorithms are made to automatically find links and patterns in the data that may not be readily apparent to people. In the case of the store owner, data mining might enable you to determine the goods that are most well-liked by particular clientele or the hour of the day when sales are at their peak.

Healthcare, finance, and marketing are just a few of the industries that might benefit from data mining. Data mining, for instance, can be used in the healthcare industry to identify people who are at risk of contracting specific disorders based on their medical history. Data mining can be used in finance to examine stock prices and forecast future trends. Data mining can be used in marketing to pinpoint the traits of customers who are most likely to purchase a specific good.

Data mining is a multi-step process. Identifying the data you need to analyze and defining the problem you want to address are the first two steps. The data must then be cleaned and put in a format that allows for analysis as the next step in preparation. This may entail cleansing the data of extraneous information, handling missing numbers, and normalizing the data.

You can start the real data mining process once the data has been prepared. In order to do this, the right algorithm must be chosen and applied to the data. The program will examine the data to find trends and connections. When the analysis is finished, analyze the findings and use them to guide your decisions.

Although data mining can be a useful tool, it's crucial to keep in mind that it can also give rise to ethical questions. Data mining, for instance, can be used to gather details about people without their knowledge or consent. Data mining must be carried out responsibly, ethically, and with regard for people's privacy.

In summary, data mining is a technology that makes use of algorithms to examine and draw patterns from big data sets. It has applications in many different fields and can be used to tackle a wide variety of problems.

Explain Data Mining like I'm five:

Finding significant information from a vast volume of data is a technique known as data mining. We utilize specialized tools and procedures to sift through the data and uncover what we're looking for, similar like digging for hidden treasure in a large mound of sand using a shovel.

Blockchain

Since its debut in 2008 as the foundation of the cryptocurrency Bitcoin, the term "blockchain" has been in use. But it has become obvious over time that blockchain has the potential to transform a wide range of businesses outside of finance. Because it has the potential to change how we transmit and store information, this technology is sometimes referred to as "Internet 2.0" or "the next internet." We will discuss what blockchain is, how it functions, and some possible uses in this explanation.

A blockchain is essentially a distributed, decentralized digital ledger that is spread across a network of computers. Each block in the chain is cryptographically connected to the one before it and contains a number of transactions or pieces of data. A block cannot be changed or removed after it has been added to the chain without the approval of the vast majority of users. As a result, the blockchain is a very safe and dependable way to communicate and store data.

Every machine in the network has a copy of the blockchain, which contributes to its security and dependability. The other computers in the network will immediately detect the discrepancy and reject the change if one computer tries to alter the data in the blockchain. Blockchain technology offers a high level of security and transparency in this way, and it has the potential to completely transform a number of industries.

The use of blockchain technology in the financial sector to power cryptocurrencies like Bitcoin and Ethereum is one of its most well-known uses. Blockchain technology is used by these digital currencies to securely and openly record transactions. Blockchain-based cryptocurrencies provide a more effective and economical means of sending money by doing away with the need for middlemen like banks and other financial institutions.

Yet, blockchain technology has many potential uses that go far beyond banking. Blockchain, for instance, can be used to generate secure digital identities that could take the place of more conventional identity verification techniques like passports and driver's licenses. As it would be considerably simpler for people to confirm their identification without the need for tangible documents, this may have a tremendous influence on everything from voting to online banking to healthcare.

Supply chain management is another area where blockchain technology may be used. Businesses may be able to improve the transparency and efficiency of their supply chains by utilizing blockchain to track the movement of goods and materials. This could lower the likelihood of fraud and corruption while also reducing waste and enhancing sustainability.

Along with these useful uses, blockchain technology has also captured the imagination of many creatives, businesspeople, and innovators. There are currently several blockchain-based art platforms that make use of the technology to produce one-of-a-kind, verifiable digital artwork. Additionally, some businesspeople are investigating how blockchain technology may be used to build decentralized social networks that would give users more control over their personal data.

In general, blockchain technology has the ability to completely change how we transfer and store data, which might have a significant impact on a variety of businesses in the years to come. Although the technology is still in its infancy and faces numerous obstacles, it is apparent that blockchain is here to stay, and the possibilities for its use are only limited by our creativity.

Explain Blockchain like I'm five:

With a blockchain, each block stands in for something significant, such as money or information, and once a block is added, it cannot be changed or removed, making the system incredibly safe and secure.

Cloud Computing

The transmission of computing services, such as servers, storage, applications, and software, over the internet is referred to as "cloud computing," a technical phrase. The metaphorical image of the internet as a cloud that inspired the word "cloud" describes how computing services are provided by distant data centers and accessible online.

Although cloud computing has been an idea for many years, it has only just become widely accepted and popular due to its many advantages, including cost savings, scalability, flexibility, and enhanced efficiency. We shall examine the several facets of cloud computing in this book, including its varieties, advantages, difficulties, and potential directions.

Based on the degree of control, management, and deployment over the computer resources, there are various forms of cloud computing. The following three categories of cloud computing:

Infrastructure as a Service (IaaS) - Through the internet, IaaS offers virtualized computer resources like servers, storage, and networking. On top of the virtualized infrastructure offered by the cloud provider, users can deploy and administer their own operating systems, applications, and software. Amazon Web Services (AWS), Microsoft Azure, and Google Cloud Platform are a few examples of IaaS providers.

Platform as a Service (PaaS) - For the creation, testing, and online deployment of web applications and services, (PaaS) offers a full environment. Users are free to concentrate on the creation and administration of their apps and services without having to worry about the supporting infrastructure. PaaS companies like Heroku, IBM Cloud, and Oracle Cloud Platform are examples.

Software as a Service (SaaS) - SaaS offers online access to software programs and services without the requirement for setup or upkeep on the user's end-user devices. Any device with an internet connection can be used by users to access the applications and services. Dropbox, Salesforce, and Microsoft Office 365 are a few SaaS vendors.

Many advantages are provided by cloud computing for people, companies, and organizations of all kinds. Several of the main advantages of cloud computing include:

Because customers only pay for the computer resources they use on a pay-as-you-go basis, cloud computing can drastically lower the costs of hardware, software, and infrastructure. As a result, there is no longer a requirement for an initial capital outlay, which also lowers the overall cost of ownership.

Without the need for extra hardware or infrastructure, cloud computing offers limitless scalability and flexibility to meet the shifting demands of the users. This gives users the flexibility to adjust their computer resources in accordance with their demands.

Because users of cloud computing can access computing resources and apps at any time, from any place, on any device with an internet connection, it can increase their productivity and efficiency. This makes it possible to operate remotely and collaborate without the need for actual devices and infrastructure.

Since the cloud providers heavily invest in security methods and technology to shield the data and applications from cyber threats and attacks, cloud computing offers improved security and data protection.

Cloud computing has numerous advantages, but it also presents consumers with a number of problems and worries.

Because data and applications are processed and kept on separate remote servers that are owned by the cloud provider, cloud computing raises questions regarding the security and privacy of the data and apps. Data breaches, data loss, and unauthorized access concerns may result from this.

Vendor lock-in can result from cloud computing because consumers may grow reliant on a single cloud provider and unable to move their data and apps to another provider or an on-premise environment.

Due to the consumers' dependence on their internet connection and the cloud provider's bandwidth, there are speed and latency difficulties. This can lead to delayed response times, network congestion, and data transfer delays.

The storage, processing, and accessibility of data and applications have all been changed by the technology known as cloud computing. It has several advantages, including cost savings, scalability, efficiency, and security, but it also has drawbacks, including concerns about data privacy, vendor lock-in, performance, and compliance. Users should keep up with the most recent trends and advancements as cloud computing continues to develop and mature. They should also carefully weigh the advantages and disadvantages of embracing cloud computing for their professional and personal requirements.

Explain Cloud Computing like I'm five:

Using the internet to store and access your data and programs is known as "cloud computing." It is comparable to having a very large computer that is accessible from anyplace with an internet connection.

Net Neutrality

The term "net neutrality" refers to the idea that internet service providers (ISPs) should treat all internet traffic equally, without making exceptions or imposing different fees on various forms of information, apps, or websites. This means that ISPs shouldn't restrict or impede access to any legitimate internet content, and they also shouldn't give some content more priority than other content for commercial or ideological reasons.

As it relates to concerns of online innovation, competition, and free speech, the idea of "net neutrality" has been the subject of discussion and contention for many years.

The concept of net neutrality has its roots in the early days of the internet, when communication and information sharing were unrestricted on an open, decentralized network. ISPs, however, started to have more control over the flow of online traffic as the internet became increasingly commercialized and consolidated, and some of them started to use discriminatory techniques that favored their own services or partners.

For instance, in the early 2000s, Peer-to-Peer (P2P) file-sharing traffic on Comcast's network was discovered to be being slowed down. Comcast justified this behavior by saying it was required to control congestion and guarantee quality of service for other users. A legal and regulatory fight over the propriety of ISPs' discriminatory treatment of particular traffic or websites resulted from this.

When the Federal Communications Commission (FCC) of the United States adopted a set of open internet principles in the middle of the 2000s, affirming the value of non-discrimination, transparency, and freedom of speech online, the idea of net neutrality attracted increasing attention. The FCC's Open Internet Order of 2010 codified these ideas and created three essential guidelines for ISPs:

1. Access to legal content, applications, services, or devices cannot be blocked by ISPs.

2. No throttling: ISPs are prohibited from slowing down or lowering the quality of legitimate traffic based on its origin or nature.

3. No paid prioritization: Internet service providers (ISPs) are not allowed to grant users access to certain content or services more quickly or with higher-quality.

These regulations were created to encourage competition, creativity, and diversity of online content and services while preventing ISPs from acting as gatekeepers or toll collectors on the internet. A large coalition of consumer organizations, internet service providers, and public interest campaigners backed them, arguing that net neutrality was necessary to preserve the internet's open and democratic nature.

Net neutrality has been the subject of numerous problems and disputes, both in the US and other nations, despite its apparent advantages and popularity.

Some detractors contend that net neutrality laws are unnecessary and harmful because they burden ISPs with excessive regulations and prevent them from expanding and enhancing their networks. They contend that consumer choice and market forces are adequate to provide an even playing field online and that government involvement will discourage competition and innovation.

Others contend that net neutrality regulations are challenging to implement and may have unforeseen consequences, like network congestion, a decline in service quality, or a decrease in the incentives for ISPs to invest in cutting-edge technology. They contend that in order to manage their networks and prioritize traffic based on technical factors like latency, packet loss, or security, ISPs must have some degree of flexibility.

Some opponents of net neutrality contend that it infringes on ISPs' and content providers' First Amendment rights because it limits their capacity to exercise editorial judgment or content regulation. They contend that ISPs ought to be free to censor or prohibit harmful or unlawful content, as well as to provide curated content or premium services that cater to their consumers' needs and preferences.

The commercial interests of ISPs and content providers, particularly smaller ones that lack the resources or market clout to compete with bigger competitors, could be harmed, according to opponents of net neutrality. They contend that permitting paid prioritization or other types of commercial discrimination would allow ISPs to increase income and make investments in better infrastructure, both of which would eventually benefit customers.

There are differences in how net neutrality rules are applied globally as well. For instance, whereas other nations have chosen a more laissez-faire approach, some have established stringent laws to preserve net neutrality. The ideals of net neutrality may have been violated by some nations' limitations on particular categories of internet content or services, such as gambling, adult content, or political speech.

Generally, the future of net neutrality is expected to be influenced by a variety of legal, legislative, technological, social, and other variables, as well as the power dynamics and stakeholder interests.

A contentious and complicated topic with numerous social, economic, and political facets is net neutrality. Net neutrality is fundamentally about maintaining the internet as a free and open platform for expression, innovation, and communication where all opinions are given an equal chance to be heard and where all users are given an equal chance to access and contribute to information and services. The success of net neutrality will depend on our ability to strike a balance between the values and interests of various parties while advancing the internet's common good.

Explain Net Neutrality like I'm five:

According to the concept of "net neutrality," ISPs should treat all websites equally, without favoring or blocking particular websites or imposing surcharges. It encourages equity, rivalry, and innovation and stops the internet from turning becoming a toll road where only the wealthy can access blazing-fast websites.

Chatbots

Using text or speech interfaces, chatbots are computer programs that mimic real-world discussions with humans. They are intended to comprehend user input in plain language and offer pertinent replies or actions in accordance with predetermined rules or machine learning algorithms. Applications for chatbots range from customer service and commerce to entertainment and education. The technology underlying chatbots, their advantages and disadvantages, and some real-world applications will all be covered in this book.

Artificial intelligence (AI) and natural language processing (NLP) technologies enable chatbots to comprehend human language and respond to it. Three key elements make up the fundamental architecture of a chatbot: input processing, dialogue management, and output production.

The steps involved in input processing include analyzing user input, figuring out the message's context and intent, and extracting pertinent entities or keywords. Many methods, such regular expressions, rule-based systems, or machine learning algorithms, can be used to do this. Some chatbots will additionally access external databases or APIs to get further context or information about the user's request.

Conversation management entails selecting the best course of action or response depending on user input and system state. Machine learning models that learn from prior encounters with users, decision trees, or predetermined rules can all be used to accomplish this. Maintaining the context and coherence of the conversation as well as resolving errors, fallbacks, and interruptions are all part of dialogue management.

A meaningful, instructive, and entertaining response or activity is what is meant by output generation. Natural language generation (NLG) methods like template-based generation, rule-based generation, or machine learning-based generation can be used to do this. Also, to improve the user experience and communicate feelings or intentions, some chatbots make use of multimedia components like pictures, videos, or emoticons.

Chatbots have advantages and drawbacks. By automating repetitive operations and responding to straightforward questions or requests, they can lower the cost of customer care and support while freeing up human agents for more intricate and individualized interactions.

Without the need for constant human presence, chatbots may offer round-the-clock support and help. This can increase client happiness and loyalty, particularly for clients who are distant or international.

Chatbots can manage numerous discussions at once without sacrificing the effectiveness or pace of the exchanges. Without the need for more resources, this can increase the capacity and efficiency of customer service and sales.

Based on the user's choices, past interactions, and behavior, chatbots can tailor the conversations and recommendations. As a result, the messages' relevancy and potency may increase, and the user experience and engagement may be improved.

Limitations include the need for complex technologies and knowledge to create, build, and maintain chatbots. They also need to be highly customized and optimized to fit the unique requirements and environments of various enterprises and consumers.

Particularly in difficult or unclear circumstances, chatbots are prone to error or misinterpretation of the user's intent or context. To enhance their effectiveness and prevent mistakes or biases, they also require ongoing monitoring and review.

Users may become wary or distrustful of chatbots, especially during private or delicate conversations. They must guarantee the privacy, security, and transparency of the data and discussions and must be completely transparent about their strengths and weaknesses.

Several businesses employ chatbots to respond to client questions, issues, or criticism on their websites, messaging services, or social media platforms. Chatbots can divert more sophisticated or individualized inquiries to human agents while giving prompt and accurate answers to frequently asked questions about things like product features, pricing, and shipping.

By engaging with users in tailored and interactive discussions, chatbots can also be used to generate leads, qualify prospects, and market goods and services. Without human assistance, chatbots can provide relevant product recommendations, offer discounts or coupons, and make bookings or transactions possible.

Chatbots can help students access and navigate online courses, respond to queries, and give comments or direction. According to the learner's performance and progress, chatbots can also offer individualized recommendations and assessments, and they can modify the course's material and pacing accordingly.

By simulating discussions with fictional characters, delivering trivia or quizzes, or making individualized recommendations for films, music, or books, chatbots can also provide users entertaining and engaging experiences. By adding fresh features or difficulties, chatbots can improve the user experience on social networking or gaming platforms.

Due to their potential to increase productivity, scalability, and user experience, chatbots are growing in popularity and becoming more commonplace in a variety of sectors and applications. To ensure their efficacy and durability, chatbots must also overcome several obstacles and limits, such as complexity, accuracy, and trust. We may anticipate seeing more inventive and creative uses of chatbots in the future, as well as more seamless and natural interactions between humans and machines, as chatbot technologies continue to develop and mature.

Explain Chatbots like I'm five:

A chatbot is a computer software that can converse with you via messaging apps, utilize AI and NLP to comprehend your questions, and provide pertinent information or take appropriate action in response. Customer support, commerce, education, health, and entertainment are just a few of the uses for chatbots. By automating processes and offering quicker service, they conserve time, effort, and resources.

Non-Fungible Tokens (NFT)

A non-fungible token (NFT) is a type of digital asset that denotes ownership or the genuineness of a special good, like a work of art, a piece of music, or a collectible. In contrast to fungible tokens, like bitcoins, which can be used interchangeably and have an equivalent value, NFTs are one-of-a-kind and have special qualities that cannot be imitated or replaced.

NFTs are built on blockchain technology, a distributed ledger that makes it possible to record and verify transactions in a safe and transparent manner. In a blockchain like Ethereum, each NFT is produced as a distinct token and linked to a particular asset or piece of content. Like to actual assets, an NFT's ownership is tracked on the blockchain and is transferable or tradable between owners.

NFTs have grown in prominence recently, particularly in the entertainment and art sectors where they provide new chances for artists and collectors to monetise and present their work. Instead of offering their works for sale as easily reproducible files, NFTs let musicians and artists sell digital versions of their works as special, precious products. Moreover, NFTs give collectors the ability to promote and exchange their collections on online marketplaces and platforms while also giving them proof of ownership and authenticity.

The digital piece "Everydays: The First 5000 Days" by artist Beeple, which sold for $69 million at a Christie's auction in March 2021, is one of the most well-known instances of NFTs. An NFT holder now owns the artwork, which is a collection of 5,000 digital photographs that Beeple produced every day for 13.5 years.

Concerns concerning NFTs' effects on the environment and their speculative character have been raised. They are accused of increasing the carbon footprint of the bitcoin sector and undermining efforts to mitigate climate change because they use a lot of energy and materials. Furthermore, several NFTs have seen significant price swings, which has prompted claims of speculation and manipulation.

NFTs are anticipated to continue developing and growing in the upcoming years despite these difficulties as more producers and collectors discover their potential and as new use cases and applications materialize. NFTs may also result in brand-new business models and sources of income for sectors outside of the arts and entertainment, such gaming, sports, and education. Like with any newly developed technology, it will be up to future development, adoption, and regulation to determine the full impact and ramifications of NFTs.

Explain NFTs like I'm five:

Unique digital assets called NFTs stand in for ownership or authenticity of things like works of art, music, or collectibles. They are immutable since they are stored on a blockchain. NFTs are well-liked in the creative and entertainment sectors, although there are worries about their environmental effects and speculative character.

Quantum Computing

A cutting-edge technology that has attracted a lot of attention recently is quantum computing, which has the potential to completely change the computing industry. Quantum computers, as opposed to classical computers, use quantum bits, also known as qubits, to process data. Quantum computers can carry out some types of calculations far more quickly than conventional computers because to these qubits. The fundamentals of quantum computing, including its principles, design, and prospective applications, will be covered in this book.

The foundation of quantum computing is quantum mechanics, which describes how matter and energy behave at the atomic and subatomic scales. Bits, which can either be 0 or 1, are used to process information in the traditional sense. Superposition is the term for the quantum phenomenon where particles can exist in several states simultaneously. This implies that a qubit can represent both 0 and 1 concurrently, enabling the execution of significantly more intricate calculations.

Entanglement is yet another crucial aspect of quantum mechanics. This happens when two particles develop a dependence between their states as a result of their correlation. This implies that even if two particles are separated by great distances, you may quickly determine the state of one by measuring the other. Entanglement is crucial to quantum computing because it enables the development of quantum algorithms that can resolve issues that conventional computers cannot handle.

Unlike conventional computers, quantum computers have a different architecture. Information is kept in bits, which can be either 0 or 1, in a traditional computer. Switches or transistors serve as the physical representation of these bits. However, data is kept in qubits in quantum computers, which can simultaneously be in a superposition of the states 0 and 1. Depending on the technology utilized to construct the quantum computer, the physical representation of qubits may change.

The use of superconducting circuits is one of the most popular methods for implementing qubits. These circuits are constructed from extremely small loops of superconducting wire, which have negligible resistance to the flow of electricity. The electrical current in these circuits can be utilized to produce qubits by cooling them to extremely low temperatures. Using trapped ions is another method of putting qubits into use. This method involves manipulating ions with lasers while they are trapped in an electromagnetic field to produce qubits.

No matter how they are made, quantum computers need sophisticated control systems to precisely manipulate and measure qubits. Because any interference or noise can quickly deteriorate the sensitive quantum states and result in processing mistakes, these control mechanisms are crucial.

The question of whether quantum computers can grow to address bigger, more challenging issues is also an issue. Even while quantum computers have produced encouraging findings for some problems, it is still unknown if they will be able to scale to handle issues that are far bigger and more complex than the ones that are being researched right now.

Notwithstanding the challenges that must be overcome, quantum computing has the enormous potential to alter computing and enhance other industries. The quick development of quantum computing research suggests that it will be operational within ten years, opening the door to novel uses and discoveries that were previously impossible with classical computers.

Explain Quantum Computing like I'm five:

Quantum computing is a new type of computer that can do certain tasks much faster than traditional computers. It uses tiny particles called qubits that can be in multiple states at once, allowing it to solve problems that would take traditional computers a very long time to solve.

Hyper Automation

Hyper automation is the practice of automating complicated business processes using cutting-edge technology like artificial intelligence (AI), machine learning (ML), robotic process automation (RPA), and intelligent business process management suites (iBPMS). This phrase is frequently used in the context of digital transformation, as businesses try to use technology to simplify and improve their processes.

In order to produce an end-to-end automation solution that can undertake difficult and repetitive activities with little assistance from humans, hyper automation incorporates a number of technologies. This can range from data processing and extraction to decision-making and action-taking. The creation of a completely automated business process with high levels of accuracy and efficiency at scale is the aim of hyper automation.

Hyper automation depends on a number of essential tools and elements that come together to build a smooth and fully automated operation. They consist of:

1. Robotic Process Automation (RPA) is a technology that enables software robots to automate repetitive and rule-based processes. RPA robots may imitate human behaviors such entering login information, copying and pasting data, and completing forms. RPA can assist businesses in automating time-consuming, error-prone, and precision-intensive processes.

2. Artificial intelligence (AI) and machine learning (ML): These two fields of technology allow for the gradual learning and performance improvement of machines. These technologies can be used to automate activities that call for judgment, including as finding trends in data, forecasting results, and generating recommendations for actions. AI and ML can also aid in process optimization by pointing up areas for improvement.

3. Intelligent Business Process Management Suites (iBPMS): iBPMS is a technology that enables businesses to structure and automate the management of their business processes. Workflow creation and management, process performance monitoring, analytics, and process efficiency insights are all possible with iBPMS solutions.

Organizations can optimize their processes and spend less time and effort completing activities with the aid of hyper automation. Organizations can give workers more time to concentrate on more difficult and strategic activities by automating repetitive and manual operations.

By automating operations that are prone to errors, hyper automation can help to lower errors and enhance accuracy. This may result in better decision-making and higher-quality results. Hyper automation can assist businesses in cutting costs by doing away with the requirement for manual labor and minimizing mistakes and rework. Organizations can use fewer resources while increasing productivity and efficiency by automating operations.

Organizations may easily and swiftly scale their operations thanks to hyper automation. Organizations can handle greater workloads without adding more workers by automating tasks.

While hyper automation has many advantages, there are also difficulties and restrictions that businesses must take into account before using this technology.

For hyper automation to work properly, data is required. The automation process might not function as intended if the data is of poor quality or not available. To ensure the data is accurate and trustworthy, firms must invest in data quality and management procedures. Many businesses use antiquated systems that are not compatible with contemporary automation technologies. Because of this, integrating new technologies into old processes may be challenging.

Hyper automation can be challenging to manage and deploy. For businesses to effectively design, execute, and maintain automated processes, they must make the necessary investments in personnel and resources. Hyper automation makes advantage of delicate information and procedures. Businesses must make sure their automation solutions are safe and adhere to legal regulations.

The future of employment is also anticipated to be significantly influenced by hyper automation. The nature of employment will change toward higher-level activities requiring creativity, problem-solving, and critical thinking as more jobs are automated. To make sure that their staff can adjust to these changes and succeed in a workplace that is fast changing, employers will need to invest in new skills and competencies.

In summary, hyper automation is a formidable technology with the ability to transform corporate processes and spur substantial advancements across a variety of industries. Although there are difficulties and restrictions to take into account, the advantages of this technology make it a viable option for businesses looking to increase productivity, save expenses, and maintain their competitiveness in the modern digital economy. We can anticipate new applications and use cases that will further alter the way we work and live as hyper automation continues to develop.

Explain Hyper Automation like I'm five:

Hyper automation is the process of automating several operations that were previously performed by people using a variety of technology, including robots and artificial intelligence. For businesses, this makes things simpler, quicker, and less expensive. By handling the monotonous and dull aspects of labor, technology can help organizations provide better customer service and make occupations more engaging for individuals. Overall, it's a really effective tool that firms may utilize to increase the effectiveness and competitiveness of their operations.

Machine Learning

Artificial intelligence (AI) in the form of machine learning enables computers to learn from experience and advance without explicit programming. It entails creating algorithms capable of data analysis, pattern recognition, and prediction or decision-making based on that data. As businesses look to use the enormous volumes of data they produce to acquire insights and improve decision-making, this technology has grown in significance over the past few years.

Creating models that can learn from data and make predictions or judgments based on that learning is the fundamental goal of machine learning. Large volumes of data must be fed to the machine learning algorithm and then used to train the model. When the model encounters new data, it will use the training it received to make predictions or choices.

The ability to utilize machine learning to automate a variety of operations that would normally require human interaction is one of its main advantages. Machine learning can be used, for instance, to automatically categorize photographs, recognize voice, or find data abnormalities. This can aid businesses in cutting expenses, boosting productivity, and enhancing the precision of their operations.

Supervised learning, unsupervised learning, and reinforcement learning are the three primary categories of machine learning. A model is trained under supervision using labeled data, where each data point is given a label or category. The trained model can then use new data to make predictions. Contrarily, in unsupervised learning, a model is trained on unlabeled data and given the responsibility of discovering patterns or associations on its own. By being rewarded for good behavior and penalized for bad behavior, a model learns through trial and error in reinforcement learning.

Predictive analytics is one of the areas where machine learning is most frequently used. Using previous data to forecast future events is known as predictive analytics. Machine learning can be used, for instance, to forecast a customer's chances of making a purchase or a patient's likelihood of contracting a specific disease. These forecasts enable businesses to make more informed choices and take early measures to reduce risks and seize opportunities.

Natural language processing (NLP), which entails instructing computers to comprehend and interpret human language, is another application of machine learning. With this, chatbots, virtual assistants, and other tools may communicate with people in a more intuitive and natural way. Machine learning can also be used to evaluate text data, such as customer reviews or posts on social media.

There are issues and limitations with machine learning, such as the need for a lot of high-quality data to adequately train models. Models that lack sufficient data may be erroneous or unreliable. Furthermore, machine learning algorithms could be difficult to understand, which can be problematic in delicate industries like healthcare or finance where decisions can have far-reaching effects.

In conclusion, machine learning is a tremendous tool that could fundamentally alter how we live and work. Organizations may acquire insights and make better decisions by utilizing the enormous volumes of data we produce. The advantages of machine learning make it a potential option for a variety of applications and sectors, despite the difficulties and restrictions to be aware of. We can anticipate new and creative use cases for machine learning to appear as it continues to develop, significantly transforming how we utilize technology to solve issues and accomplish our objectives.

Explain Machine Learning like I'm five:

Machine learning is a type of computer intelligence that enables machines to learn and improve from experience without being programmed explicitly. Essentially, it involves teaching computers to recognize patterns in data and make predictions or decisions based on that learning. This technology can help automate many tasks that would typically require human intervention, leading to increased efficiency and better decision-making.

Cybersecurity Mesh

Modern technology must include cybersecurity, which is becoming more and more important as we rely on technology to store and handle private data. The demand for strong cybersecurity safeguards is only going to increase as the internet of things (IoT) grows. Cybersecurity mesh is a relatively new idea in the field of cybersecurity, and it promises to give enterprises in numerous industries improved protection.

A cybersecurity mesh is essentially a network of connected security products and services created to safeguard a company's digital assets. A cybersecurity mesh's objective is to offer a more adaptable and decentralized security infrastructure that can handle the ever-changing security environment. Its distributed architecture enables security to be integrated wherever it is required, increasing its adaptability, dynamicity, and scalability.

Security is centralized and delivered by a set of security instruments that are controlled by a specialized security team in a traditional cybersecurity approach. But the old strategy is no longer sufficient with the rise of connected devices and cloud services. The decentralized model of cybersecurity mesh substitutes the centralized strategy. To create a thorough security posture, it depends on security services that are dispersed across the enterprise, connected, and orchestrated.

A cybersecurity mesh offers a more flexible and adaptable approach to security, which is one of its main advantages. It can safeguard IoT, mobile, and cloud services in addition to more conventional IT assets. This is so that security can be provided at the data level independent of where or how access to the data is made possible.

A cybersecurity mesh also has the benefit of enabling security to be built right into programs and services, leading to a more secure-by-design strategy. This method lessens the chance that security flaws will be included later in the development process and can assist firms in meeting legislative obligations like the GDPR or CCPA.

A cybersecurity mesh can be hard to construct, though. Interoperability is one of the most difficult problems.

A cybersecurity mesh necessitates the coordination and interconnection of numerous security services, which can be difficult and complex to accomplish. Organizations must also make sure they have the knowledge and experience needed to operate and sustain a distributed security architecture.

In summary, a cybersecurity mesh is a distributed design that makes it possible to incorporate security wherever it is required. It offers a more adaptable, granular, and flexible approach to security, which makes it appropriate for safeguarding contemporary technology infrastructures like IoT, cloud services, and mobile devices. Although putting in place a cybersecurity mesh has its problems, the advantages make it a desirable alternative for businesses trying to strengthen their security.

Explain Cybersecurity Mesh like I'm five:

A cybersecurity mesh is a network of security services that guards a company's digital assets, such as cloud services, IoT, and mobile devices. It provides flexible security that is tailored to the unique requirements of each asset. A cybersecurity mesh's implementation, however, might be challenging and call for a variety of interconnected security services and knowledge.

Sustainable Technology

Sustainable technology is the application of technology to the production of goods and services that are both socially and environmentally responsible and commercially profitable. It includes a variety of technological advancements, such as clean technology, renewable energy, and green infrastructure. Sustainable technology aims to maximize the positive effects of technology while minimizing its negative effects on society and the environment.

The usage of renewable energy sources is one of the fundamental components of sustainable technology. Solar, wind, and hydroelectric power are examples of renewable energy technologies that provide electricity without consuming natural resources or harming the environment. We can lessen our dependency on fossil fuels and cut greenhouse gas emissions, which contribute to climate change, by using renewable energy.

Another crucial aspect of sustainable technology is clean technologies. Clean technologies aim to reduce negative environmental effects and increase resource efficiency. Examples include electric vehicles, energy-efficient structures, and sustainable agricultural methods. By boosting productivity and generating new jobs, they also provide economic advantages.

The utilization of natural systems and processes to deliver ecosystem services, such as flood control, water purification, and carbon sequestration, is known as "green infrastructure" and is another aspect of sustainable technology. Wetlands, woods, and green roofs are a few examples of green infrastructure.

Specific technologies, sustainable design, and sustainable consumption are all included in sustainable technology. Sustainable design entails producing goods and services that are both socially and economically viable as well as environmentally sustainable. Consuming products and services sustainably means reducing the negative effects on the environment and fostering social responsibility.

The understanding that conventional technologies have had detrimental effects on the environment and society is one of the fundamental forces behind the creation of sustainable technology. These detrimental effects include resource depletion, pollution, and climate change. We can reduce these negative effects while still utilizing the positive aspects of technology by creating and implementing sustainable technology.

Adoption of sustainable technology has several obstacles, nevertheless. Cost is one of the key obstacles. Sustainable technologies, especially those that use renewable energy, might be more expensive than conventional ones. It could be challenging for companies and individuals to accept them because of this. Sustainable technology is, however, becoming more affordable and available to a wider range of individuals as a result.

The necessity for technological innovation is another difficulty. Continuous research and development are needed to provide new and improved technologies that are more effective and efficient. For firms and governments, this might be difficult because it calls for a sizable investment in research and development.

Notwithstanding these difficulties, sustainable technology has several advantages.

We can lower our greenhouse gas emissions and lessen the effects of climate change by using fewer fossil fuels. We can reduce waste and lessen our impact on the environment by incorporating sustainable practices into every aspect of our life. Also, we can encourage social responsibility and build a more sustainable future for all by supporting sustainable businesses and products.

In light of the threat of global warming and the need to cut greenhouse gas emissions, sustainable energy is becoming more and more significant. Globally, sustainable technologies like wind, solar, and geothermal energy are becoming more affordable and widely available. Although there are still issues with infrastructure and policy, people, businesses, and governments must cooperate for a sustainable and prosperous future.

Explain Sustainable Technology like I'm five:

In order to create and use technology in a way that is long-term beneficial to society and the environment, it must be sustainable. Using sustainable resources, such as wind and solar energy, and creating items that can be recycled or reused are examples of this. Finding ways to fulfill our needs without endangering the environment or future generations is the overall goal of sustainable technology.

Internet of Things (IoT)

The network of physical objects, including machinery, transportation, home appliances, and other goods, that have sensors, software, and connectivity built in to allow data exchange over the internet is known as the Internet of Things (IoT). In other terms, it refers to the idea of internet-connected devices that can speak with one another and with people. The IoT has grown in popularity over the past several years as a result of its ability to alter numerous industries and increase production, efficiency, and convenience.

Although the idea of the Internet of Things has been around for a while, recent technological advancements have made it more practical and available. Now that low-cost sensors and wireless connectivity are more widely available, practically any device may be connected to the internet and data can be gathered from it. Processes may be strengthened, performance can be tracked, and decisions can be made using data analysis.

The ability to gather and analyze data from a variety of sources is one of the IoT's most important advantages. For instance, sensors in a plant may track the efficiency of tools and machinery, keep tabs on energy use, and spot possible problems before they get out of hand. Similar to this, sensors may monitor energy use, regulate temperature and lighting, and offer security features in a smart home.

The capacity to automate operations and lessen the need for human interaction is another benefit of the IoT. For instance, when a homeowner leaves their smart house, gadgets can automatically change the temperature, turn off the lights, and lock the doors. Machines in a factory can communicate with one another to increase productivity and decrease downtime.

New goods and services have been created as a result of the IoT. Wearable technology, such as smartwatches and fitness trackers, may track activity and health and offer individualized recommendations. A smartphone app can be used to remotely operate smart home appliances like thermostats and security systems. Moreover, IoT technology is being employed in the transportation sector to increase productivity and security, such as in self-driving cars.

The ability to gather and analyze data from a variety of sources is one of the IoT's most important advantages. For instance, sensors in a plant may track the efficiency of tools and machinery, keep tabs on energy use, and spot possible problems before they get out of hand. Similar to this, sensors may monitor energy use, regulate temperature and lighting, and offer security features in a smart home.

The IoT, however, also presents a number of difficulties and dangers. The challenge of protecting data privacy and security is one of the major issues. With so many devices connected to the internet, there is a risk of hacking and data breaches. Additionally, there is a risk of data being used for unethical purposes, such as tracking people without their consent or sharing personal information without permission.

The interoperability of gadgets and systems is another problem. It can be challenging to make sure that they can all interact and function together seamlessly given the variety of devices and protocols. This may cause compatibility problems and impede the creation of new goods and services.

Also, concerns regarding the IoT's effects on employment and jobs are raised. There is a risk of job loss and economic disruption as more processes are automated and machines take over duties previously performed by humans. Finding solutions to reduce potential negative impacts and taking into account the social and economic ramifications of the IoT are crucial.

In summary, the Internet of Things is a quickly developing field with the potential to revolutionize numerous industries and enhance ease, productivity, and efficiency. Yet it also presents a number of difficulties and dangers that need to be handled. It is essential to make sure that technology is applied responsibly and ethically as the IoT spreads and technology advances. As part of this, it's important to handle security and privacy issues, ensure interoperability and compatibility, and take into account the IoT's social and economic ramifications.

Explain Internet of Things like I'm five:

IoT is the term used to describe a network of physical items, including machines, cars, buildings, and other things, that are connected to the internet and equipped with sensors, software, and connections.

Business Intelligence

Corporate leaders, managers, and other stakeholders can make better decisions by using business intelligence (BI), a technology-driven process of data analysis and presentation. It incorporates a collection of tools and methods for converting unprocessed data into valuable insights that may be utilized to spot trends, patterns, and chances to boost business performance.

BI involves gathering, storing, and analyzing data from a variety of sources, including market trends, social media, corporate transactions, and consumer interactions. After processing, the data is turned into useful information that can be utilized to support business choices through reports, dashboards, and visualizations.

One of the main advantages of BI is that it helps businesses understand their operations and the market they compete in better. They can use this to find growth opportunities, streamline company operations, and come to more wise conclusions. A business might, for instance, utilize BI to examine sales data to determine which products are selling well and which are not. They might decide on pricing, marketing, and product development tactics based on this information.

Through the automation of procedures and the reduction of the time and labor needed for data analysis, BI may also be utilized to enhance operational efficiency. BI technologies can assist firms in identifying issues and taking corrective action before they worsen by supplying timely and accurate information. This can help businesses save time and money, which helps their bottom line.

A typical BI system has a number of important parts, including data warehousing, data mining, reporting, and analytics. In data warehousing, a vast volume of data is gathered and stored from numerous sources in a central repository so that it can later be accessed and examined using BI tools. Analyzing data to find patterns and relationships that can be used to forecast the future and guide business decisions is known as data mining.

Reporting is the process of putting facts into an understandable format that can be applied to help decision-making. These could include tables, graphs, and charts that illustrate important developments and conclusions. Analytics is the practice of analyzing data using mathematical and statistical models in order to anticipate future trends and results.

Self-service BI, one of several types of BI technologies available, enables users to design their own reports and visualisations utilising data from numerous sources. Additional BI tools come in the form of dashboarding tools, which offer a real-time view of important performance measures, and predictive analytics tools, which analyse data and forecast future trends using machine learning algorithms.

Notwithstanding these difficulties, BI has several advantages. BI may help firms make better decisions and perform better overall by giving them access to timely and accurate information. The need for BI tools and services is anticipated to continue to increase as data becomes more crucial to businesses of all sizes.

In conclusion, business intelligence is an essential tool for companies looking to understand their business processes and make data-driven decisions. Companies may gather, store, analyse, and visualise data from multiple sources with the use of BI tools to gain a complete picture of their business performance. Moreover, BI can assist businesses in identifying trends, spotting opportunities, and reducing risks.

Explain Business Intelligence like I'm five:

Business intelligence (BI) is the umbrella term for the technology, tools, and procedures used by businesses to gather, integrate, analyse, and present data in a way that aids decision-making. BI enables businesses to collect data from numerous sources, translate it into information, and produce insights that can be put to use. Organizations can enhance their operations, cut costs, and find fresh growth prospects by utilising BI.

Metadata

Information that describes other data or information is referred to as metadata. It is simply information about information, giving more context and specifics about the information it is describing. Data organisation, discovery, and use all depend heavily on metadata, which is a vital part of data management.

Metadata come in many forms, and they can be divided into three groups: descriptive, structural, and administrative. The data's title, creator, and subject matter are just a few examples of descriptive metadata that are used to characterise the data's content. The format and arrangement of the data, such as the file format and the way the data is set up inside a file, are described using structural metadata. Administrative information, such as the creation date, version number, and access permissions, are used to administer the data.

The management of digital material, such as images, movies, and music, as well as libraries, archives, and museums, all frequently make use of metadata. Metadata has grown in significance over the past few years in the world of technology, especially in fields like data analytics, artificial intelligence, and the internet of things.

Metadata is essential for analysts and data scientists to comprehend the data they are working with in the context of data analytics. Metadata can assist analysts in making better educated judgements about how to evaluate and interpret the data by providing more context and information about the data. Metadata, for instance, can assist analysts in determining the data's origin, the time frame it covers, and any pertinent data quality issues that need to be taken into account.

As it enables machine learning models to learn from massive volumes of data and generate predictions, metadata is essential to artificial intelligence. By spotting biases or inaccuracies in the data, metadata makes sure that the data used to train models is accurate and pertinent to the task at hand.

Metadata is used in the internet of things (IoT) context to assist in managing the enormous amounts of data produced by IoT devices. IoT devices can produce a lot of data in real time, and metadata is used to provide the data more context and specifics, such the device's location, the time it was collected, and the kind of sensor it was collected from. Organizations can then utilise this metadata to manage and analyse the data more efficiently, allowing them to make better decisions based on the data produced by their IoT devices.

Generally, metadata is crucial to technology and data management. It aids in giving the data context and specifics, making it simpler to organise, find, and use. Data analytics, artificial intelligence, and the internet of things are just a few of the many applications that employ metadata. Metadata is crucial to the efficient administration and use of data in various areas.

Explain Metadata like I'm five:

Metadata is information about other data. It is data that provides context to other data. It can help you understand what the data is, where it came from, who created it, when it was created, how it was created, and other useful information.

Search Engine Optimization (SEO)

The process of improving a website or online piece of content for search engine results pages is known as search engine optimisation (SEO) (SERPs). The search engine algorithm determines which websites and pages are the most pertinent and helpful for a given query when visitors enter a certain keyword or phrase. By making a website more valuable and relevant to visitors, SEO tries to raise a website's ranking in these results pages.

Keyword research, on-page optimisation, technical SEO, and link building are a few of the approaches and tactics used in SEO. The process of optimising content entails finding the keywords and phrases that are pertinent to a given website or piece of content through keyword research. In order to improve a website's search engine friendliness, on-page optimisation entails improving its content and architecture. This entails optimising the content itself as well as the page names, meta descriptions, and header tags.

Technical SEO entails enhancing a website's technical components to raise its search engine rating. This entails enhancing a website's performance and speed, adding schema markup to aid search engines in understanding a website's content, and making sure the website is mobile-friendly.

To increase a website's authority and relevance, link building entails obtaining high-quality backlinks from other websites. This can be accomplished using a variety of strategies, including influencer outreach, broken link construction, and guest blogging.

Because search engines drive the majority of web traffic, SEO is crucial. Being highly ranked in search engine results can therefore greatly improve website traffic and potential clients. Due to the fact that visitors are more likely to trust websites that are at the top of search engine results pages, it can also increase brand visibility and credibility.

Yet, SEO is a field that is continuously developing, and search engine algorithms are no exception. As a result, it's critical to stay current on the latest SEO best practises and adjust techniques as necessary. Furthermore, there is a chance of using unethical or spammy SEO techniques, which can lead to fines or even complete exclusion from search engine results pages.

The exposure, traffic, and reputation of a website can all be dramatically impacted by SEO, which is a crucial aspect of internet marketing. It entails a range of tactics and methods targeted at enhancing a website's authority and relevance in search engine results pages. Nonetheless, it's crucial to keep up with the most recent best practises and steer clear of dishonest or spammy methods.

Explain SEO like I'm five:

Search engine optimisation, or SEO. It is a collection of methods and tactics used to increase the visibility of websites and their position on search engine result pages like Google, Bing, or Yahoo. This is significant because the majority of people utilise search engines to locate the information they are seeking for online.

Edge Computing

In contrast to transferring data to a centralised data centre or cloud, edge computing processes data locally, at the point of origin. This method can offer real-time analysis and insights while cutting down on the time and bandwidth needed to transport data to a central location for processing. We shall examine edge computing's definition, operation, and uses in this book.

The fundamental idea behind edge computing is to move processing power closer to the locations where data is generated and gathered. To do this, computing resources are placed at or close to the edge of a network, such as at the location of an Internet of Things (IoT) device, a sensor, or a machine. As a result, data may be processed, examined, and used immediately without having to be sent to a distant data centre or cloud.

As the number of sensors and connected devices increases and the demand for real-time data analysis and insights rises, edge computing is becoming more and more popular. Also, edge computing can lessen bandwidth utilisation and network latency, which can be especially helpful in applications where data needs to be handled fast and effectively.

The ability to enable novel applications and services that conventional centralised computing architectures cannot is one of the main advantages of edge computing. Edge computing, for instance, can be used to enable real-time monitoring and control of machinery in a factory or to give drivers on the road real-time traffic information. Since sensitive data can be processed locally rather than being transferred over the open internet, edge computing can also be utilised to improve security and privacy for that data.

Fog computing, mobile edge computing, and decentralised computing are only a few of the various technologies and methods used in edge computing. These strategies differ in their areas of concentration and application, but they all aim to bring computer power closer to the places where data is produced and gathered.

The fact that managing edge computing might be more difficult than with conventional centralised computer systems is one of its drawbacks. This is due to the fact that maintaining computing resources deployed across many distinct locations, as is the case with edge computing, can be more challenging than managing resources in a single centralised data centre or cloud. A larger spectrum of companies will now be able to more easily utilise edge computing thanks to the development of new tools and technologies.

Applications-wise, edge computing has numerous possible use cases in a variety of industries. For instance, edge computing can be used in manufacturing to continuously monitor and improve production operations, resulting in higher productivity and efficiency. By using edge computing in the transportation industry, drivers can receive real-time traffic updates and have their routes optimised, which will ease traffic and increase safety. Edge computing in healthcare can be used to continuously monitor patients and deliver individualised, targeted therapies based on personal health data.

Edge computing, as a whole, is an innovative and quickly developing field of technology that has the potential to revolutionise a variety of sectors and applications. Edge computing enables novel applications and services that were not feasible with conventional centralised computing architectures by moving computer resources closer to where data is generated and gathered. Before implementing edge computing, organisations must carefully assess their needs and capabilities because, like any new technology, there are difficulties and complexity with edge computing.

Explain Edge Computing like I'm five:

The term "edge computing" describes a technology that enables the proximity of computing resources, such as storage and processing power, to the location where data is generated. This is in contrast to conventional cloud computing, which involves the processing and storing of data in centralised data centres that are situated far from the point of production.

The book "Crack the Tech Code: A Simplified Guide to Technology Terminology" aims to make difficult technological words easier for people to comprehend. The book covers a wide range of topics, including internet jargon, security, programming languages, hardware, and software for computers. Each topic is covered in detail, with straightforward language and understandable examples that make it easier for readers to comprehend even if they are unfamiliar with the subject. Also, the book offers helpful hints and recommendations to keep readers abreast of the most recent technological trends and advancements. Overall, "Crack the Tech Code" is a helpful tool for anyone wishing to increase their awareness of and familiarity with technology.

Crack the Tech Code:
A Simplified Guide to Technology Terminology

By Alex Imm

Cover design by Alex Imm.
ISBN 9798389040823.
This book is a work of non-fiction.
For permission to reproduce any portion of this book, please contact the author at tookay.nn@gmail.com.

First edition.

Crack the Tech Code:
A Simplified Guide to Technology Terminology

By Alex Imm

Printed in Poland
by Amazon Fulfillment
Poland Sp. z o.o., Wrocław
10 August 2023

325743f3-f801-4b76-8f44-6315e3564a6cR01